14·46

INTERDISCIPLINARY STUDIES FROM THE SCANDINAVIAN SUMMER UNIVERSITY

Editorial Board

Vol. III

HUMANITIES PRESS . NEW YORK

INTERDISCIPLINARY STUDIES
FROM THE SCANDINAVIAN SUMMER UNIVERSITY

RAGNAR ROMMETVEIT

ACTION
AND
IDEATION

Explorations into some interrelationships
between conviction, attitude
and behavioral choice

HUMANITIES PRESS

NEW YORK

HUMANITIES PRESS, Inc.
Publishers and Distributors of Scholarly Books,
303 Park Avenue South, New York 10, N.Y.

Published simultaneously
in Denmark by Munksgaard, Copenhagen

Printed in Denmark by
A. Backhausens Bogtrykkeri, Horsens

EDITORIAL FOREWORD

The Scandinavian Summer University, established in 1950, is dedicated to the pursuit of interdisciplinary discussions and studies. It brings together students and scholars from Denmark, Finland, Iceland, Norway and Sweden in an effort to further scientific cooperation and counteract the narrowness of mind and onesidedness of approach which is often the result of increasing specialization in the realm of higher education and in scientific research.

Each summer the institution holds a two-weeks' session in one of the Scandinavian countries. A central subject is chosen for the work of each year. At the summer session ten to fifteen study-groups work on different aspects of this subject; in addition lectures and round-table debates take place. During the spring term there are arranged at the ten Scandinavian universities study-circles in which the participants prepare for the summer meeting.

A series of yearbooks, each embodying the work of one of the years 1951 to 1956 and 1958, has been published in the Scandinavian languages. The present series attempts to represent the work of 1957, 1959 and the following years in a somewhat different manner. Instead of one large volume, a number af smaller volumes are published each year. The authors are usually persons who have taken a leading part in the work either in the spring or the summer session and who afterwards have undertaken to write about a topic in the treatment of which they have contributed. Their task has not been to report what went on in the study group or the plenary session concerned but to present their own views on the topic in question after it has been tested and modified in the discussions.

The main subject for 1959 was "Knowledge, Valuation and Choice". The summer meeting took place at Frederiksborg in Denmark. At one of the plenary sessions, the recently appointed Professor of Psychology at the University of Oslo, Ragnar Rommetveit, gave a lecture on the psychology of convictions and conversions. The present volume contains a much revised and expanded version of that lecture.

MOGENS BLEGVAD

CONTENTS

I

INTRODUCTION

From the time of antiquity philosophers have discussed rational and irrational aspects of human behavior. The doctrines of Hedonism and Egoism emphasized irrational determinants of man's conduct. Machiavelli did not believe in attempts at appealing to people's intellect, nor did Hobbes think highly of Man's ideational guidance and control of action. The Enlightenment, however, seemed to have as its very core a rather profound confidence in "the command of reason". Then another devaluation emerged from Freud's penetrating studies, and in particular from his discovery of ideational misrepresentation or camouflage of irrational acts.

Is it true, then, that my ideas are frequently most adequately interpreted as intellectual superstructures upon irrational acts, or do they as a rule initiate and control my behaviors? To what extent and under which conditions will my conviction be influenced in an irrational way? And what happens under conditions of obvious discrepancy between action and ideation, for instance when I am forced to act in a way contrary to my ideology?

Such general questions suggest the direction of our explorations. We shall venture to go into a jungle of largely unexplored problems, searching for fragments of recent psychological theories and findings of relevance for our understanding of them.

II

IMPLICIT RATIONALISTIC ASSUMPTIONS
IN RESEARCH ON SOCIAL ATTITUDES

Some of the general problems indicated above may perhaps be illuminated by social psychological research, and in particular by the social psychologist's study of *social attitudes*. A characteristic feature of an attitude is "a state of motive arousal" (19, p. 118). According to most definitions, furthermore, it has an essential emotional component as well. In brief, attitudes may be defined as enduring predispositions to be motivated and emotionally involved in a characteristic way in relation to parts or aspects of our physical and social world, e. g., one's own nation, a political party, a national or racial group of people, etc.

Ordinarily, however, a man's attitude is "measured" in terms of a recording of verbally expressed opinions and convictions (10). In the well-known California studies of authoritarian and ethnocentric attitudes (1) for instance, an authoritarian attitude toward children is attributed to people who are convinced that it is more important to teach children respect toward authority than showing them affection and love. By the same token, a hostile attitude to toward minority groups is inferred when an individual maintains that Negroes and Jews should live in isolation and under strict control.

If, then, on the one hand we define attitudes as predispositions to act and be emotionally involved, while on the other hand, in our empirical studies we actually infer such predis-

10

positions from recorded opinions and convictions, we are immediately faced with a series of problems concerning the relationship between ideology and conduct. Will the person who considers respect for authority the most important educational goal actually treat his children in an authoritarian way? And the individual maintaining that minority groups should be isolated and strictly controlled – does he act in a hostile way toward members of minority groups? In short, what can social psychologists tell us about correspondence between verbally expressed conviction and behavioral choice?

Even though carefully controlled empirical evidence bearing upon this issue is meager, some attempts have been made at examining the relationship between attitude (as inferred from verbally expressed opinion) and actual behavior. Thus, people's religious attitudes have been examined and related to their church-going practices (25) and political attitudes have been checked against voting behaviors. In most such "validation studies" a fairly high, albeit far from perfect, correspondence has been observed. On the other hand, we are faced with demonstrations of striking discrepancies like the classical study by La Piere (16). He accompanied a Chinese couple on some of their travels, and later questioned the managers of the restaurants, hotels, and auto camps that they visited. Most of them informed him that they would not accept Chinese guests, though all of them had in fact done so.

Such discrepancies have naturally aroused the social psychologist's interest, and various sources of discrepancy have been thoroughly discussed in methodological studies (10, 13). Thus, our attention is directed toward sources of error inherent in the social psychologist's assessment of convictions. In some cases, for instance, the interviewee may yield to the temptation of overt compliance with widely held and socially accepted opinions. To the extent that his private convictions deviate from a socially accepted pattern, they may be more or less suppressed and concealed in the interview. If so – and under

11

a number of similar conditions – we are probably faced with an *apparent* discrepancy between ideation and action. The observed discrepancy is, upon a more thorough investigation, simply recognized as an artifact due to inadequate assessment of "true" opinions.

Cases of genuine discrepancy between ideology and conduct may sometimes be explained in equally simple and trivial ways. The young man with an ardent radical attitude may secretly vote conservative in order to restore his peace of mind after a traumatic fight with his conservative father, and the convinced pacifist is voluntarily enrolled in the army after all because of a strong suspicion that his pacifism may be weakness and cowardice. Likewise, the atheist living in a religious environment may go to church on Sundays simply to please his neighbours. In such cases, strong motivational predispositions consonant with an intellectual conviction seem to be successfully counteracted by internal and external inhibitions.

The examples and interpretations above suggest an outlook on the relationship between action and ideation that seems to be tacitly adopted in a number of studies of social attitudes: The intellectual conviction, as revealed in written or spoken statements, is implicitly considered an essential cognitive component of the attitude itself and as such conceived of as a powerful determinant of action. When reaction tendencies "caused" by such a conviction are inhibited, discrepancy between ideology and conduct is observed. But such a discrepancy is then considered an exception confirming the rationalistic rule. Overt compliance contrary to the conviction (e. g., the atheist's churchgoing) may actually be based upon a careful ideational representation of, and choice among, alternative behaviors and possible outcomes. It may be considered *unethical*, but by no means does it testify against "the command of reason" in human behavior.

12

Psychologists emphasizing rational aspects of man's attitudes thus tend to view ideation as an integral part of a more inclusive and unitary cognitive, motivational and emotional structure. The attitude is defined (15, p. 152) as "an enduring organization of motivational, emotional, preceptual and cognitive processes ...". In their analysis of attitude change, furthermore, they frequently draw our attention to a characteristic temporal pattern. As a rule, they argue, perceptual and ideational changes occur prior to changes in emotional and motivational predispositions (19, p. 218).

III

DISCOVERY OF COVERT RATIONAL PATTERNS IN APPARENTLY IRRATIONAL OPINION CHANGE

One of the most outstanding spokesmen for such a rationalistic outlook on attitude and opinion change is Solomon Asch, a German psychologist who settled in the United States and in continuous experimental research at Swarthmore College accumulated a large and impressive body of evidence in favor of "the command of reason". In some of his earlier studies (2) Asch wanted to reexamine a set of phenomena ordinarily referred to as "prestige suggestion". According to previous investigations, opinion change due to prestige suggestion appeared to be abrupt and "blind" in the sense (3, pp. 255) "that *an unchanged object of judgment undergoes change of evulation*". The essential features of the experimental findings were traditionally described as follows:

(A) The subject is faced with an isolated object of judgment, e. g., the statement T_o, which leads to the evaluation X.

(B) A source of high prestige $(P+)$ is introduced, i. e., T_o is presented as a quotation from a speech by the authority $P+$.

(C) When T_o is thus brought into contact with $P+$, the evaluation X is changed so as to agree with $P+$. Concretely: An individual admiring Eisenhower accepts and endorses an opinion about American foreign policy he previously rejected once he is informed that the opinion is held by Eisenhower.

From careful experimental studies and postexperimental interviews with his subjects, however, Asch arrives at the conclusion (2, p. 462) that "… standards imputed to congenial groups produced *changes in the meaning of the objects of judgment*".[1] His findings thus do not seem to testify to irrational compliance with the authority. On the contrary: an essential feature seems to be a rational reinterpretation of the statement in a new context, and the apparently "blind" change of opinion is accordingly described as follows:

(A) The subject is faced with an object of judgment, the statement T_o, which *in isolation* is interpreted as meaning T_i and leads to the evaluation X.

(B) A source of high prestige (P+) is introduced, i. e., T_o is presented as a quotation from a speech by the authority P+.

(C) In view of this information, T_o is interpreted as meaning T_j, i. e., as expressing *an opinion more consonant with the subject's expectations with respect to P+ than was* T_i.

(D) The subject then indicates his agreement with T_j, i. e., with *an opinion he did not read into T_o at all at stage (A)*. Concretely: The ardent Republican accepts and endorses an opinion about American foreign policy he did not read into the statement at all until he was informed that the statement had been made by Eisenhower.

Similarly, in his more recent experimental studies of the effect of majority pressure upon individual judgment, Asch is repeatedly faced with an apparently irrational change of conviction (4). The individual usually seems to abandon a firmly held and *correct* judgment when all other group members unanimously maintain a false opinion contrary to simple sensory evidence. In some of the studies, all but one subject are paid participants who are instructed to give false judgments of length of lines. Even though line A is slightly shorter than line B, they repeatedly – throughout a series of judgments – maintain that B is shorter than A. After a while the naïve subject, believing that all others are actually perceiving B as

[1] Italics ours.

15

shorter than A, usually appears to abandon his correct judgment in favour of compliance with the others.

Even in this experimental version of Hans Andersen's "The Emperor's New Clothes", however, Asch succeeds in drawing our attention to essentially rational patterns of behavior. In intensive interviews after the experiment, the naïve subject's overt compliance is frequently disclosed as deliberate "lip service". Actually, the subject is still privately convinced that line A is shorter than B, and has been so all the time. In the experimental setting, however, he only pretended to agree with the others for the sake of peace or social acceptance or some other easily understandable (though possibly opportinistic) reason. Other cases of compliance seem to reflect genuine, even if "rational" modifications of *judgments*. Prior to his compliance the naïve subjects then seems to have reasoned as follows: "I am convinced that line A appears shorter to me than line B. Since all the others are of a different opinion, however, there may be something wrong with my vision. I had therefore better rely upon the unanimous judgment of the rest of the group rather than in my own subjective experience". Thus, upon a more thorough investigation, nearly all cases of "blind compliance" are actually identified as disguised rational patterns of the kinds suggested above.

IV

IRRATIONAL CHANGE OF ATTITUDES
AND CONVICTIONS
UNDER GROUP PRESSURE

The picture of the rational man implicit in studies of social attitudes and emerging from reexaminations of authority and majority suggestion, however, seems to be seriously challenged by recent investigations of "group dynamics". Whereas Asch presents us with an impressive amount of evidence in favor of "the command of reason", Leon Festinger and other students of group dynamics have conducted numerous carefully planned laboratory experiments and field studies by which clearly irrational aspects of man's ideation in a social context are brought into focus (6, 8).

First, their findings seem to provide us with fairly conclusive evidence of genuine opinion change under conditions of social pressure. In a group of people, they assume, there will arise pressures toward uniformity, i.e. (6, p. 272) "pressures which ... act toward making members of a group agree concerning some issue or conform with respect to some behavior pattern".

One major source of such pressures, furthermore, seems to be the individual's emotional and motivational investment in the group. He may join a group for a variety of reasons, i.e., in order to achieve social acceptance and experience human sympathy, because of his attraction to specific activities requiring interaction in a collectivity, etc. Irrespective of the main direction of his motivational orientation, however, his participation in group life seems to have obvious instrumental aspects. Therefore, *individual opinions and convictions may also be viewed as embedded in a complex means-ends structure.* Certain opinions are apparently instrumental in the achievement of group- and individual goals, others may be clearly detrimental. In general, then, deviant opinions seem to be modified so as to agree with a collective pattern. And the more intensely a member wants to remain in the group, the greater is the prize he may be induced to pay for it in terms of genuine opinion change.

In some cases, such an opinion change may be entirely rational, in the sense that the individual simply reorganizes his outlook on an issue on the basis of significant and valid information provided by other members of the group. The essentially irrational component, however, is brought into focus when it is shown that the persuasive effect of a given item of information is actually dependent upon the recipient's affiliation to the group. This seems to be corroborated both by field studies and laboratory experiments in which the relationship between group cohesiveness and uniformity of opinions is examined. Referring to these findings, Festinger therefore ventures to maintain (6, p. 277) that *"the amount of change in opinion resulting from receiving a communication will increase as the strength of the resultant force to remain in the group increases for the recipient"*.

Reminding ourselves of the "disguised rational patterns" in the studies by Asch, however, we may still be somewhat unwilling to accept the observed correspondence between group cohesiveness and uniformity of opinions as definite evidence of genuine opinion change. Initially at least, the individual may comply *overtly* in order to be accepted by the others and conceal an unchanged private opinion deviating from the group norm. The question is, however, whether such a deliberate and rather self-conscious strategy will be adopted at all when strong and possibly unconscious motives are at stake, e. g., when the individual apparently is not aware of the urgent need for social acceptance underlying his compliance. Secondly, opportunistic "lip service" may possibly develop into genuine opinions *over time*. This actually seems to happen in "natural" groups. A member who initially reluctantly complies may after some time be observed eagerly persuading others to accept the majority opinion.

When interpreting such phenomena, Festinger draws our attention to another major source of pressures toward uniformity of opinions in a group. The opinion of other group members, he maintains, constitute a *"social reality"* against which the validity of my own subjective outlook is tested.

In many cases, I am able to test the validity of a conviction and achieve subjective certainty by means of a direct sensory contact with the reality to which my conviction refers. I am of the opinion that it is raining outside and know for certain that I am right when I stretch out by hand and feel the raindrops against my skin. My opinions regarding such issues as the political system in China or juvenile delinquency, however, cannot be validated in such a simple way. Hence, when the opportunities of testing the validity of my conviction by simple sensory contact with a physical reality are severely reduced or nearly non-existent, I am almost entirely dependent upon the "social reality" surrounding me in my attempts at finding out whether I am right or wrong. My own conviction is checked against those of my friends and authorities. As a rule, the more others agree with me, the more certain I feel. When I learn that all my friends share my outlook and find that the editor of my daily newspaper corroborates my conviction as well, then I may even be prepared to maintain publicly that I *know* I am right. My feeling of subjective certainty, developed under the influence of those very friends and authorities, has then emerged into an illusion of objective and "true" knowledge. As raindrops against my skin unequivocally confirmed my opinion about the weather, so may a social reality unequivocally confirm my outlook on a social issue.

Such considerations seem to be of particular relevance in attempts at explaining the exceptionally high stability and group conformity with respect to political, religious and moral convictions. Because of his need for subjective certainty and lack of opportunities for unequivocal validation via simple sensory contact, the individual tends to seek out other people and choose among other potential social stimuli (in mass media, for instance) in such a way that *he exposes himself to a strongly biased "social reality"*. When his opinion is challenged by relevant information, moreover, he may actually begin seeking additional social support for his challenged opinion rather than make use of available means for a more direct sensory control of its validity.

In addition, the interaction observed *within* the small group seems to reflect a feedback mechanism securing group consensus. In brief, direction and amount of communication appear to be determined partly by individual deviance from the group norm. The member expressing a deviant point of view will immediately have an extraordinarily large amount of communications directed toward him, and such persuasive efforts are usually continued until he is "brought back" to compliance with the majority opinion. Again, we are reminded of the significance of our need for subjective certainty. When I am eagerly persuading the deviant, I am actually at the same time trying to restore my own faith. His deviance represents a crack in the otherwise compact and unequivocal social reality upon which the phenomenal validity of my own conviction depends.

In our analysis of the stability of religious and political convictions we should also take into consideration potential effects of strong emotional involvements. When faced with new pieces of information, items that are consonant with our con-

20

victions apparently tend to be more easily perceived and re-called. This has been corroborated in a number of experimental investigations (17, 26), and alternative theoretical explanations have been suggested. In most cases the relative dominance of attitude-consonant items in perception and memory is probably due primarily to our familiarity with them rather than an emo-tional interference in purely cognitive processes. I remember well, in a discussion, the arguments of a member of my own party, simply because I was already acquainted with such view points. On the other hand, I do not recall my political op-ponent's contributions in that discussion very well, since my perception and retention of his statements were not facilitated to the same extent by previous acquaintance with them.

Irrespective of the kind of theoretical explanation offered, however, selective learning and retention may be justly con-ceived as integral links in a complex *circulus vitiosus* by which an initially weak opinion is continually reinforced and con-firmed in a social reality. I subscribe to the paper supporting my point of view, testing its validity against the opinions of those who agree with me. Only infrequently do I expose myself to information contrary to my outlook, and such information is then hard to understand and easily forgotten. In short, I am living in a very stable social world, structured in terms of my firmly held convictions and validated against a social reality.

V

THE TENDENCY TO REDUCE DISSONANCE
IN ACTION AND IDEATION

By assuming that social reality is a major source of pressure toward uniformity, students of group dynamics also invite us to make an interesting reexamination of persuasion and proselyting behaviors. We may have some reasons to expect that, as a rule, ardent propagandists would be strongly convinced of the validity of their ideolygy. If we persuade others in order to increase or restore our own faith, however, particularly vigorous proselyting behaviors should occur under conditions of extreme doubt and uncertainty.

This derived hypothesis seems to be supported by the findings from a most interesting field study by Festinger, Riecken and Schachter (9). They decided to investigate a rather peculiar recent religious movement in the U.S.A. In order to do so, they entered the small group of believers themselves. Being accepted as ordinary members of the sect, they were able to follow a most interesting chain of events from within, as participating observers. As a result, accurate and detailed records of the activities of the group were kept. And the climax was enacted one chilly December night when all the members were gathered, waiting for flying saucers to arrive and transport them to other planets.

According to the prophecies of the sect leader, a cataclysm was soon going to take place. The believers would be safely picked up by the flying saucers, they were informed, and most of them had already made detailed preparations for the departure. However, after four days of breathless excitation and expectation – from December 17th to 21st – they were forced to realize that the prophecy had failed. During those four days there were three specific and unqualified disconfirmations and a strong attack at the key points in their ideology. Some members were then obviously disillusioned and disappeared from the group. Those who did not abandon their beliefs, however, appeared to be somewhat reassured by the leader, who claimed that she had received a message informing her that the catastrophe had been called off. And now followed a peculiar change of attitude toward proselyting. After having described the secrecy and passivity characteristic of the group's life up to the crisis, the participant observers continue (9, pp. 213):

"In sharp contrast, intense proselyting activity characterized almost every member of the group following disconfirmation. For the first time in her prophetic career Marian Keech initiated telephone calls to the newspaper. Bertha Blatsky, in dread of her husband, had desperately avoided publicity before the 21st. On the morning of 21st, she talked to reporters, released the secret tapes, and promised to record tapes for anyone who asked – including the National Broadcasting Company. Mark Post telephoned a number of the newspapers and was interviewed by several reporters ... Cleo Armstrong had done her utmost to avoid reporters ... After disconfirmation Cleo lectured to reporters and boldly argued with them about the validity of the belief system ... After disconfirmation, proselyting became the popular pastime."

These carefully controlled observations of the ways in which the believers responded to categorial disconfirmations of the prophecies draw our attention once more to man's need for subjective certainty. When there is a strong commitment to a conviction, significant factual evidence may apparently be ignored and easily explained away. The individual's need for security then seems to precede his need for veridical cognition: serious doubt due to evidence contrary to the conviction is "drowned" in increased social support. In short: We seem to seek *safety and harmony* more than *truth*. This, in brief, seems to be one of the basic theses in Festinger's theory of cognitive dissonance (7).

According to Festinger's recent theoretical formulations, there is in man a basic need for harmony in action and ideation. This need is revealed in persistent attempts at reducing conflict or *cognitive dissonance*, he maintains. When new information goes contrary to my previous knowledge, when there is an obvious discrepancy between my actions and my ideology, when two of may convictions are mutually contradictory, etc. – in all such cases we are faced with a state of cognitive dissonance and a resultant need to restore harmony.

When, therefore, the ardent believer realized that no flying saucers nor cataclysms arrived, a state of profound dissonance followed. Unequivocal and significant facts clashed with strong expectations constituting the cornerstone of his religious ideology. Two major kinds of solution were then in principle available. The believer might abandon his beliefs, or he might try to restore harmony and subjective certainty by means of ingenious reinterpretations of disconfirming events and increased social support. As we have seen, both kinds of dissonance-reducing strategies were apparently adopted.

The theory of cognitive dissonance has also served as the theoretical basis for a number of experimental investigations. Some of the latter are actually experiments on corruption. The subject is induced – by reward or threat of punishment – to act contrary to his convictions. After having participated in an extremely tedious and boring psychological experiment, for instance, he is paid to persuade another student to volunteer as a subject in the same experiment. In order to do so, he is actually forced to describe the experiment as interesting, i.e., in a way contrary to his own genuine opinion. Afterward – and in a completely different context – he has the opportunity to express his own genuine opinion about the experiment. The important question is then whether the forced compliance – the fact that he has tried to persuade another person in a way contrary to his own conviction – has produced an opinion change.

According to the experimental findings,[1] such a genuine opinion change does seem to occur. The magnitude of the change, however, seems to be inversely related to that of the reward – or punishment – by which the compliant behavior has been induced. Thus, when the student is paid only one dollar for persuading another student to participate in the boring experiment, he afterwards reveals, as a rule, a clear-cut tendency to glorify the experiment when freely expressing his opinion about it. If he has been overpaid, however, i. e., receiving 10 dollars in reward for his corrupt action, his poor opinion of the experiment apparently remains by and large unchanged. The explanation is, according to Festinger, that the poorly paid corruption – because of the *obvious discrepancy between the seriousness of the compliant act and the price by which it was induced* – sets the stage for cognitive dissonance. After the corruption, the individual is forced to realize that he has publicly acted against his own convictions, and he is unable to justify this unhappy state of affairs by referring to magnificent rewards or serious punishment. The corrupt act, furthermore, cannot be undone nor explained away. The individual then seems to modify his convictions so as to *reduce dissonance between present ideation and past acts.*

Concretely: The student who at a price of one dollar only has been induced to glorify the tedious experiment and persuade another student to volunteer as a subject, apparently cannot accept and live with the fact of such a cheap corrup-

[1] Some of these studies have not yet been published. My summary account of them is largely based on lectures by Dr. Festinger.

tion. Nor is he able to ignore the corrupt act. His ideation then seems to take the following course: "The experiment was perhaps not so extremely boring after all. Now I come to think of it, there were actually quite interesting things in it ...". The overpaid student, however, may probably restore his peace of mind by reasoning along the following lines: "Of course, the experiment was extremely boring. But ten dollars are quite a bit of money. Anybody would fake a bit of enthusiasm for such pay, so I haven't any reasons to blame myself ...".

The investigations of the ways in which induced compliance affects ideation thus seem to provide us with fairly clear evidence testifying to subtle irrational cognitive mechanisms. First, they show that, under certain conditions, forced compliant *behaviors* actually lead to covert modifications of *opinions*. Secondly, they suggest that there is an optimal value of the price for corruption: maximal opinion change follows when the reward or the threat of punishment is barely sufficient to induce compliance. Excessive sanctions (as, for instance, the means by which an occupation army frequently forces the conquered people to comply) apparently tend to reduce the state of cognitive dissonance following corruption and consequently also the potential *ideological change* initiated by forced compliance.

VI

NOTES ON ALTERNATIVE CRITERIA
OF "RATIONALNESS"

The reader may now have the impression that our explorations have led us back to our point of departure, without having provided us with any clear answers to the naïve and general questions we asked. Before exploring into other fields, we shall therefore reexamine our *formulations of the problems* in the light of the fragmentary empirical evidence encountered so far.

First, from studies of social attitudes and reexaminations of suggestion, there emerged a picture of the individual who *acts* and *is emotionally involved* in a rational way. The intellectual conviction seems to be a powerful determinant of behavior *per se*, and apparently "blind" changes in the person's emotional and behavioral dispositions toward some aspect of his world are, upon careful examination, identified as logical consequenses of a preceding purely *cognitive* change. In short, ideation initiates and controls action.

Students of group dynamics, however, directed our attention toward the anchorage of convictions in *a social reality*, emphasizing various manifestations of *a need for subjective certainty* in opinions and outlook on the world, a need that appears to be stronger than our desire to know the truth. Sometimes, it seems, I may actually conquer my own corroding disbelief by persuading others to accept and share my badly challenged belief. And my firm intellectual conviction, it seems, may even be modified by forced behavioral compliance and in such a way as to become more consonant with my corrupt actions.

By combining these major fragments of a picture of man which emerge from recent social psychological investigations, we seem to end up with a composite picture of a distinctly Janus-faced being. Upon further inspection, however, we soon realize that our picture is still very ambiguous and incomplete. In our discussion of attitude change, for instance, a temporal pattern of *ideational change preceding modification of emotion and motivation* was interpreted as evidence for "the command of reason". But are we really justified in doing so, *without taking into consideration the determinants of the initial ideational change itself?* It may for instance be proved that I did not start buying a new brand of tea until I got to know about specific qualities of that brand that I had not thought of before. Still, my friends may argue that I certainly would not have been so easily convinced about these qualities if it had not been for the personal charm of the salesman who told me about them.

On the other hand, we may have reasons to ask whether anchorage of convictions in a social reality *per se* is irrational. My opinion on an issue may have developed on the basis of opportunistic compliance. If "the others" on whom I have relied *are* right, however, should my opinion be then labelled "irrational" merely because of its indecent genesis? If I knew from the very beginning that they were experts on that issue, compliance would actually simultaneously gratify my need for veridical knowledge as well as "opportunistic" desires for social acceptance, etc.

By raising such questions we realize the need for a further clarification of notions of "rationalness" implicitly accepted in our explorations hitherto. We have several times encountered *temporal patterns* of ideation-action relationships of some relevance for judgment of rationalness of behavior. "The command of reason", we have assumed, is revealed in ideation prior to action, and in an attitudinal *change* that, initiated by new information, via a modification of cognition finally penetrates "down" into emotional and behavioral dispositions. The reversed pattern, i.e. the penetration of emotional and behavioral dispositions into ideational processes, has been considered irrational.

In our discussion of these phenomena, however, we have carefully avoided explicit criteria of rationalness. Moreover, since we have been primarily concerned with ideation-action *relationships*, little has been said about rational and irrational aspects of *single acts and opinions*. Because of our preoccupation with problems of causality, i. e., ideation *causing* action, motivation *influencing* ideation, etc., we have also largely ignored *simultaneous ideation and action* characteristic of "self-conscious" behavioral processes. Sometimes, overt behavior and thought processes actually seem to merge in such a way that I am at a given moment unable to decide whether the present idea represents an anticipation of my next action or a memory of the immediate past. In such cases, I may tell my friends *what* I am doing and *why* I am doing so *while I am acting*, and such an account of the behavior taking place may then upon closer examination turn out to be false and directly misleading. Again, my conduct may be considered irrational, but now in the sense that there is a discrepancy between *an action taking place* and *my ideational representation or introspective account of it*.

When now trying to summarize the essential features of the various phenomena labelled "irrational" according to our naïve notions, we shall start out with single opinions and acts and then proceed to complex ideation-action relationships.

An *opinion* or a *belief*, then, may ideally be confirmed or falsified by testing it against "the true state of affairs". If, for instance, I am of the opinion that Germans are hostile, that opinion can *in principle* be judged as "true" or "false" in the sense that *it may be unequivocally transcribed into a prediction of the outcome of specific psychological investigations.* As naïve realists, we may thus conceive of percepts and ideas as rational and irrational in the sense that they *correspond to or are discrepant with external realities.*

Such an absolute criterion of rationalness, however, does not seem very helpful in a psychological diagnosis of "the command of reason". Even if my opinion about the hostility of Germans should turn out to be veridical, it may have developed on the basis of opportunistic compliance with uninformed anti-Germans. In order to get at genuinely psychological aspects of rationalness, we shall therefore probably have to search for criteria other than correspondence between cognition and "truth".

We are then immediately brought back to intricate problems of genesis and causality encountered in psychological studies of compliance and dissonance reduction. In such studies, we found that, as a rule, the opinion is not validated at all against the external reality to which it refers. Instead, it is examined *as an end-product of the individual's previous experiences,* and irrationalness is accordingly diagnosed by investigations of *opinion formation.*

Such genetic strategies for assessment of rationalness have been repeatedly and ardently opposed by people who are afraid of "psychologism". Instead of fighting my opponent by means of arguments referring to the issue under discussion, I may question his motives or capacities. And if no objective criteria of "rational opinion formation" exist, even the research psychologist may sometimes run the risk of accusing Man of irrational conduct because he discovers patterns of opinion-formation violating his own private and ideosyncratic ideals of the rational man.

In view of these considerations, we are tempted to search for criteria of *rational opinion formation* analogous to the absolute criterion for *veridical cognition.* Suppose that we knew my complete life history. Imagine, furthermore, that all my experiences were carefully coded and clearly transcribed into bits of information. These bits of information might then be fed into an electronic computor whose task would be to provide us with the correct conclusion with respect to some issue. Finally, my own opinion might be compared with the computor's answer to the problem.

Such a procedure of investigating rational opinion-formation can be considered, we feel, roughly analogous to the procedure by which the truth of an opinion may be assessed. Both strategies actually refer to imaginary processes by which the logically sound inference from a complex set of bits of information is achieved. In both cases, furthermore, we are faced with the problem of screening irrelevant bits of information. If data are fed into the computor in a temporal order corresponding to the order in which they actually were potentially available to me, a correction for memory loss may even be introduced. Considering opinion as an end-product of organization of experiences, then, we actually try to assess its rationalness by checking it against the end-product of a process of strictly logical inferences. Rationality then seems to imply *isomorphy between the human mind and a computor operating according to some logical calculus*. At least, *discrepancy* between my opinion and the computor's solution to the problem may be used as a criterion for *irrational* opinion formation. And a rational opinion may therefore be tentatively defined as *an inference by which the information provided by previous experience is maximized*.

Such criteria of rationalness implies that man's "command of reason" is seen against the background of his restricted experience rather than against an "objective reality". If essential bits of information have never been available to me, I may have developed a *rational*, though *false*, outlook on some aspect of my world. On the other hand, obvious deviance from the hypothetical logical pattern of inference may be discovered in studies of opinion formation even though the *end-product* turns out to be a *veridical cognition*.

We may now briefly reexamine some of the evidence for such deviance and – if possible – specify a few major irrational *strategies*. A person complies with others in order to achieve some important personal goal. He modifies his conviction so as to restore his self-respect and peace of mind after forced behavioral compliance. After unequivocal disconfirmation of expectations, he may even start persuading others in order to restore his own faith.

In all these cases, we feel, there appears to be a common denominator of *"bad intention"*. Whereas the computor is given the unequivocal and single task of arriving at the correct answer, formation of opinion in man is apparently often subject to interference from other important activities taking place. Opinions may be embedded in inclusive means-ends-structures and are probably then partly formed and changed according to rules other than those of the logical calculus. Once the computor is given a bit of information such as, for instance, a specific argument of relevance to my opinion about Germans, it does not care whether the argument was presented by an influential person or an underdog. If they are equally well-informed and trustworthy, the impact of that additional bit of information upon the computor's answer to the problem will be zero. Its impact upon my opinion, however, may be considerable. In short, my friend the computor is a truth-seeker by profession, whereas *my* cognition may obviously also serve needs other than a desire for truth.

Secondly, opinion formation occurs in a genuinely social setting. Even though I may be ardently seeking the truth and nothing but the truth, the opinions of people sorrounding me apparently present a "social reality" against which the veridicality of my own opinion is continually checked. If all members of my clique agree with me on an issue, this fact obviously represents information of relevance to my conviction. Other things being equal, the probability that I am right will increase in proportion to the *number of people agreeing with me* × *their probable competence with respect to the issue concerned*. This, in principle, is the way in which group consensus would be fed into the computor.

As a human being, however, I do not respond to the members of my clique merely *qua informants*. Their opinions are – as mine – end-products of organization of experiences. In the terminology of our computor analogy, therefore, significant "others" acquire the status of *other computors against which the end-product of my own calculation is continually checked*. This, in short, seems to be the essence of their status as my social reality. Merely because of their psysical proximity and my interaction with them, my uninformed neighbors and friends gradually acquire the status of reliable computors of the truth concerning racial issues in the United States, whereas the opinion of an outstanding expert on those very issues enters my experience as *another bit of information* only. Our friend the computor, on the other hand, is superior and *asocial* by profession. He has no friends and neighbors, nor any equals at all. Therefore, no bit of information is interpreted by him as a message representing another reliable computor's answer to the problem on which he is working.

Thirdly, deviance from the computor's supreme rationalness may simply be due to incapacity. The computor, being a professional genius, makes no errors of calculation. I may seek the truth and nothing but the truth and – hypothetically – even do so independently of any social reality. If I am simply unable to perform the mental operations corresponding to the logical operations required for a correct solution, however, I am still bound to fail. The extremely irrational man is therefore the person whose opinions serve urgent needs other than his desire to know the truth, who is highly dependent upon others in his outlook on the world, and, moreover, stupid.

In brief, irrationalness defined as deviance from our hypothetical compu&or's *opinion formation* seems to branch off into a triumvirate of *bad intention, sociability,* and *stupidity.*

If we now consider *the single act,* however, this typology of deviance from a hypothetical rational pattern seems hardly appropriate at all. First, the important aspect of an act seems to be its *instrumentality* rather than its *veridicality.* In order therefore to find out whether an act is rational or not, we have to examine it as *a means toward some goal.* Accordingly, irrationality *qua sin against the ideal of absolute truth-seeking* drops out. By the same token, extreme behavioral compliance can hardly be considered irrational *per se.* Instead of acting "according to his own desires", an individual may apparently choose a mode of behavior agreeable to his companions. If so, however, it may possibly be shown *post facto* that his *"real goal"* was social acceptance, or that the strongest motive behind the act was avoidance of ostracism, etc. In order to assess the rationalness of a single act against our friend's the computor's choice of behavior, we thus have to make, *a priori,* specific assumptions concerning the desired outcome of that act.

Once we are willing to make those assumptions, however, we are in principle able to compare my choice of behavior with a decision representing maximal use of information provided by previous experience and made in accordance with some logical calculus. By doing so, we again avoid an "experimenter-centered fallacy" in assessment of rationalness. My act will be considered rational in relation to my previous experience even when it does *not* represent the optimal choice of behavior under the ideal conditions when all relevant bits of information were known to me.

In order to suggest some rather interesting implications of such a criterion of rationalness of behavioral choice, let us now imagine the following situation of decisionmaking under uncertainty:

An individual is faced with a choice between three actions,

a_1–a_3. Whatever he does, he runs the risk of losing some money. The magnitude of his loss, however, is dependent upon his choice and a future state of nature. He knows that one of two different states of nature, S_1 and S_2, may occur, but he is entirely ignorant with respect to the probabilities of S_1 and S_2. Let us assume, then, that he is faced with the *loss matrix* below. If he chooses action a_1 *and* S_1 occurs, he will lose 200 dollars. If a_1 is chosen and S_2 occurs, he will lose nothing at all, etc.

	S_1	S_2
a_1	200	0
a_2	168	48
a_3	120	120
(a_4)	(0)	(300)

Let us assume, furthermore, that *the individual's major aim is simply to safeguard himself against great regret afterward.* In other words, he wants to choose a mode of behavior *"minimizing maximal regret"* (23). For that purpose, the loss matrix is transformed into a regret matrix. If he chooses a_1 and s_1, occurs, the regret will be 80 dollars, i. e. his regret will then be that of having lost 80 dollars more than if he had chosen a_3, which is *the optimal behavioral choice provided that S_1 occurs.* The regret matrix under conditions of these behavioral choices will therefore be as described below, and his aim of safeguarding himself against great regret is securely achieved by choosing action a_2. By that choice he does not risk a regret greater than 48 dollars at all, whereas a_1 and a_2 imply risks of regrets of respectively 80 and 120 dollars.

	S_1	S_2
a_1	80	0
a_2	48	48
a_3	0	120

If now our individual has been misinformed in the sense that he believes that a fourth behavioral choice (a_4 in the loss matrix) is available, his regret matrix will be significantly changed. The amounts of post-decision regret he is now faced with will be as as shown in the following regret matrix.

Under these conditions, therefore, a_3 will be his logical choice. In other words: *His choice among three possible actions has been influenced by the introduction of an additional irrelevant alternative, even though the latter is not chosen at all.*

	S_1	S_2
a_1	200	0
a_2	168	48
a_3	120	120
a_4	0	300

According to our suggested criterion of rationalness of acts, then, his choice of a_3 is *rational*. The fact that he has been misinformed is clearly irrelevant in this context. Once it is shown that a_4 actually was perceived by him as an available behavioral choice, it should also be fed into the computor as a bit of information of relevance to his choice.

The simple example above may possibly open up a new outlook on apparently "peculiar" decisions. Often, when we conceive of acts as "irrational", their essential characteristic seems to be *deviance from "the normal mode of behavior"*. Furthermore, if a person chooses a_3 while I and all my friends prefer a_2, I am sometimes led to the conclusion that he is stupid, or I may feel that he is narrow-minded and *"does not see"* a_2. Seldom does it occur to us that he may actually make a perfectly *rational choice*, a choice, however, that appears strange to us simply because we do not share his enriched outlook on behavioral alternatives. Actions that appear peculiar and irrational may thus upon a more thorough investigation actually be identified as *end-products of entirely rational strategies applied to particularly rich human experiences.*

Even if they are considered end-products of rational *strategies*, it does not follow from the criterion we suggested that rational acts have to be *initiated* and *controlled* by conscious ideation. A person's choice of behavior in a given category of situations may be repeatedly observed to coincide with the computor's rational choice, even though his own introspective account of behavioral choices makes it clear that he has been acting all the time "without foresight". This seems to be the essence of *"rational intuition" in human conduct.*

The latter term may appear paradoxical in view of some aspects of rationalness we emphasized in our previous explorations. The priority of reason revealed in the rationalistic psychologist's study of Man was apparently in part reflected in a temporal pattern of conscious ideation prior to action. The rational behavioral choice, according to this point of view, would therefore have as an essential characteristic *foresight*, i. e., it would by definition be a choice based upon conscious inference. If people act without knowing their reasons they are, we feel, *eo ipso* behaving in an irrational way.

Suppose, then, that we repeatedly observe two persons, Mr. X and Mr. Y, in a category of choice-situations. Both persons have the same aim, we assume, and for the sake of simplicity we also assume that they have had exactly the same experiences of relevance to the solution of the problem. If now Mr. X *spontaneously, without knowing his reasons for it,* chooses a mode of action a_j coinciding with the computor's logical choice whereas Mr. Y chooses each time *after a series of elaborate conscious inferences* some action category a_i that does obviously *not* represent an optimal and logically sound use of the information provided by his previous experience, which person is then behaving in an irrational way?

Obviously, the fact that a person *"has ideas"* of relevance to the behavioral choice prior to his action does not guarantee at all that his decision will be logically sound. Nor does absence of conscious ideation prior to the act prove the absence of (preconscious or unconscious) mental operations corresponding to the computor's subtle and logically stringent operations. As a matter of fact, *our friend the hyper-logical computor is itself operating intuitively in the sense that it is unable to give an introspective account of anticipated and ongoing activities.* We may of course try to put "self-consciousness" into it by providing it with additional mechanical devices. Thus, if a particular operation such as, for example, *simple addition*, invariably leads to a certain rise of temperature in one particular part of the machine, a gadget may be introduced in such a way that local temperature rise automatically activates a tape record playing "I am adding".

By providing the computor with "insight" and "hindsight" in such ways, however, we do not interfere with its "intuitive" reasoning at all. We merely build into it an additional mechanism corresponding to what Nuttin (20, p. 352) labels "reflective consciousness" or "consciousness raised to the second power", i. e., an awareness and recording of one's own mental operations at the time they are being performed. Even if it is not essential for the computor's operations, however, such reflective consciousness seems to be an essential property of the *human* mind. Its relevance to the understanding of our problems, furthermore, appears obvious once we shift our focus from single acts and ideas and study rationalness from the angle of man's cognition of his own overt actions and internal processes. Man is rational, we feel, when he has self-insight. And, fortunately, his account of his reasons for a choice may be correct even though the choice itself proves irrational occording to our former criterion. On the other hand we may encounter logically sound *behavioral choice without self-insight*, i. e., genuinely *intuitive* actions repeatedly and consistently coinciding with the computor's foolproof recipe for achievement of some important goal.

Even this criterion of *self-insight* seems to imply a surplus of moral judgment. Irrationalness then means *deviance from an ideal of knowing the truth about oneself.* Accordingly, it may be due to sin, sociability, and stupidity, i.e., our cognition of own acts may be flavored by motives other than a desire for veridical self-insight, we may be unduly influenced by other people's explanations of our behaviors, and we may not have the capacity required for arriving at the logically sound cognition.

Furthermore, if we elaborate and combine the criteria of *self-insight* and *optimal use of information provided by previous experiences,* we shall probably arrive at an extremely complex set of criteria of rationalness. A case of perfectly rational conduct, i.e., a pattern fulfilling both criteria of rationalness, would then be *a behavioral choice representing an optimal and logically sound use of information provided by previous experience, initiated and accompanied by a conscious inference in such a way that the mental operations governing the choice are adequately represented in the person's "reflective consciousness".* Genuine discrepancies between ideation and action of the kind encountered in attitude research, however, may possibly sometimes be identified as patterns fulfilling only one of our criteria. In our further explorations we shall return to one interesting category of such discrepancies, namely *the rational act accompanied by irrational ideation.*

VII

A PSYCHOANALYTIC APPROACH
TO OUR PROBLEMS:
PRIMARY AND SECONDARY
MENTAL PROCESSES

If we now reconsider the evidence pro and contra rationalness in Man we have encountered in recent social psychological studies, some rather interesting patterns seem to emerge. In short, evidence pro rationalness seems to have been accumulated by and large in settings in which man is faced with *problems of cognition per se*, whereas evidence pro irrationalness stems largely from experimental settings in which *cognition appears to be instrumental toward some superordinate individual goal*.

Thus, in the studies of opinion change and judgments of length by Asch, the individual's task is explicitly or tacitly *defined* as that of arriving at a "correct" conclusion or judgment with respect to some issue. In the studies by Festinger and associates on small group processes and forced compliance, on the other hand, cognitive processes seem to be embedded in complex means-ends-patterns. The individual's major intentions are then apparently geared toward goals other than veridical cognition, and he has no reason to anticipate that his judgments or opinions afterwards will be examined with respect to their validity.

Irrationalness defined in terms of deviance from truth-seeking is, therefore, apparently dependent in part upon purely situational factors, i. e., the experimenter is able to enhance "sin" simply by introducing cognitive tasks as integral parts of a complex sequence of behaviors, e. g., as means serving some significant personal need. Rationalness, on the other hand, is apparently enhanced under conditions of induced "reflective consciousness", i. e., when the individual's awareness is directed toward cognition *per se* and toward the veridicality of his own cognitions rather than some superordinate behavioral goal. The pattern emerging from our survey of social psychological studies therefore seems to testefy to the significance of the psychoanalytic distinction between *primary and secondary mental processes*, i. e., between *cognition under the regime of the pleasure principle* and *cognition governed by and oriented toward reality*.

Schafer (24, p. 77) describes these two modes of cognitive organization as belonging to "different levels of functioning", and he continues:

"Secondary process thinking is predicated upon delay of immediate, direct, unmodulated discharge of influences; it seeks such detours toward gratification as are appropriate to the individual's total prevailing life situation; it is selective and modulating. Also, secondary process thinking is oriented toward reality and logic, it is reflective and forward-looking; it maintains the boundaries between self and not-self. Primary process thinking, in contrast, is indifferent toward reality and logic and is organized around the vicissitudes of drives; it is oriented toward immediate, direct, and uncontrolled discharge of impulse; it is fluid, undiscriminating, and unreflective; it ignores relations of time, place, identity and causality. In addition, primary process thinking tends to fuse self and not-self; and it teems with condensations, displacements, psysiognomic impressions and magical notions."

According to Schafer, then, primary processes – being governed by unconscious motives – are by definition beyond reflective consciousness and voluntary control. When thus an individual feels excitement and disgust after forced compliance contrary to his conviction, a "fusion of self and not-self" may

41

occur in the sense that *a need to restore self-respect* of which he is not aware at all "teems with" *memory of the corrupt act* and *ideation referring to the issue concerned.* In a way, primary processes then seem to break through so as to modify cognitions that otherwise would be "oriented toward reality and logic". Similarly, an unconscious need for subjective certainty may possibly penetrate into perceptual processes in such a way that an argument against my point of view is partly experienced as an attack on my personal integrity and prestige. In general, primary processes seem to break through and blur "pure reason" whenever my ideation and action are governed by impulses *whose very existence and manifestations remain unknown to my reflective consciousness.*

In deliberate opportunism, on the other hand, my reflective consciousness seems to penetrate into may opportunistic motives themselves. When I am aware of the fact that I am striving toward some goal such as, for example, social acceptance, the boundaries between self and not-self are maintained in the sense that *I am able to distinguish between "truth" and the issue as viewed from my particular motivational orientation.*

Reflective consciousness thus implies that I "become an object to myself", as George Herbert Mead (18) puts it. The opportunistic need does not then enter my experience as a vague feeling of tension and striving only. If correctly diagnosed by myself, it also enters *secondary processes* as a veridical and significant bit of information. Once I am aware of my "bad intentions", therefore, it seems as if I may actually *prevent* or at least to some extent *correct for* their interference with my logical reasoning.

In this respect, reflective consciousness *in Man* obviously serves significant purposes other than an exact recording of ongoing mental activities. It represents a state of awareness in which my own personal desires, being detached from my cognition of external phenomena, become a focus of cognition themselves. This orientation, furthermore, seems to enhance an ideational organization geared toward communication. I view the world and myself in such a way that I am in principle prepared at each stage to verbalize and report on my cognitions. This continuous conceptualization of present impressions and past experience is then apparently in turn a *sine qua non* for a process of conscious and logically stringent inference.

An *irrational opinion*, on the other hand, may, as previously suggested, be identified in some cases as the product of a fusion between an unconscious desire and a cognition of some "external reality". As such, it is a bastard of Pleasure and Truth like the neurotic's and psychotic's serious distortions of reality. Furthermore, when we consider the hypothesized dominance of unconscious motives in the neurotic's interaction with his environment *in general*, we have reasons to expect that personalities with symptoms indicative of acute neurotic conflicts will manifest a greater deviation from a hypothetical rational pattern than others when exposed to influences of relevance to *opinion change*. Because of the neurotic's unconscious motivational investment in his outlook on the world, his reactions to new information are supposed to be characterized by rigidity and excessive resistance to cognitive change.

These expectations seem to be partly corroborated in an experimental study by Janis (14). In brief, his subjects were exposed to a series of communications without being aware of the fact that the experimenter actually was interested in observing opinion change. The experimental session was represented as an "oral speaking test" for vocational guidance purposes. The communications resembled the newspaper editorials which give a slanted presentation of factual arguments in an attempt to convince the audience of certain beliefs and expectations, namely, that *movie theaters would go out of business* as a result of television and other recent developments, that *total meat supply in the U.S. would decline rapidly*, and that *an effective cure for common cold would be discovered very soon.*

Prior to this camouflaged persuasive influence, a variety of personality characteristics of the subjects had been assessed by means of personality inventories and available clinical reports. Furthermore, by comparing the individual's opinions on the three issues before and after the experiment, the impact of the communications upon opinion change was assessed. Finally, observed variations in susceptibility to persuasion could be traced back to individual differences with respect to such personality characteristics as "neurotic anxiety symptoms", "obsessional symptoms", "inhibitions of aggression", etc.

The results – though far from conclusive – reflect some fairly unequivocal trends in support of the hypothesized rigidity and excessive resistance to cognitive reorganization in the neurotic personality. In general, individuals with symptoms of anxiety and obsession turned out to be very resistant to change. Extremely *high* susceptibility to persuasion, on the other hand, was observed in individuals with feelings of social inadequacy, inhibitions of aggression, and depressive affects. And both excessive resistance and extreme compliance apparently represent deviance from a hypothetical rational pattern of response to the persuasive communications. In view of these findings, therefore, the author arrives at the following tentative conclusions (14, p. 516):

"... symptoms of acute neurotic anxiety might be associated with the presence of defensive inhibitions which interfere with efficient use of intellectual and judgmental capacities. Even among nonneurotic persons who fall well within the 'normal' range of personal adjustment, those who display disturbances similar to the acute symptoms of severe neurosis would presumably be somewhat less likely than others to function efficiently in communication situations. In such individuals,

44

defense mechanisms, emotional blocks, and generalized anxiety reactions are likely to interfere with attention, comprehension, and acceptance of persuasive communications".

According to psychoanalytic theory of primary and secondary mental processes, furthermore, the essence of *rationalization* seems to be *an apparently rational ideational superstructure upon an irrational act or reaction tendency*. We tend to "dream up" plausible accounts and explanations of acts initiated by desires and cognitions beyond the scope of our reflective consciousness and voluntary control. Since such acts are considered products of primary mental processes, they are in general supposed to be "indifferent toward reality and logic". When judged against our criterion of *logically sound and in all respects optimal use of information provided by previous experiences*, rationalized acts should accordingly stand out as particularly significant evidence pro irrationalness in human conduct.

The *rationalization itself*, however, may often appear rational from certain points of view. If we assume that a person's "genuine" reasons for a given act cannot possibly be assessed by his reflective consciousness, we may study his account of it as an interesting instance of problem-solving or behavioral choice. His task may then be defined as that of offering a "plausible" or "acceptable" explanation of an apparently peculiar event, *irrespective of the "true" causal texture*. He may for instance have a choice between a number of explanations of which only *one* has a plausibility sufficient to prevent serious embarrassment. When making his choice, furthermore, he may possibly anticipate and include in his calculations a variety of different potential reactions by others to alternative explanations of the acts, etc. In short, his rationalization of the act is obviously rational in the sense that secondary rather than primary processes seem to be involved. It may even prove rational in the sense that it represents *the optimal solution of his problem*, i. e. an optimal use of information provided by his previous experiences in service of some temporarily important motive, such as, for instance, the prevention of embarrassment.

Pregnant examples of such rational superstructures upon irrational acts are frequently encountered in reports on post-hypnotic phenomena. The hypnotized individual is told, for instance, that a few minutes after having awakened he is going to open the window. And he does so, apparently without being aware of the fact that he is obeying a command, however, and with the seemingly plausible explanation that it is hot or smoky in the room. His account of the compulsory act is then apparently rational, i. e., it seems to represent a logically sound derivation from his rather firmly based knowledge of the *most likely* – and *eo ipso least embarrassing* – reasons for opening windows in such situations.

VIII

"RATIONAL INTUITION" IN PERCEPTION
AND INTERPERSONAL RELATIONS

From Schafer's description of primary and secondary processes and our excursions into rationalizations and posthypnotic phenomena we may get the impression that optimal use of information provided by previous experiences presupposes *reflective consciousness*. Acting without foresight, however, does not occur only on the couch and after hypnosis. If we consider the multitude of acts and behavioral choices performed throughout a single hour of our everyday busy life, we may well arrive at the conclusion that reflective consciousness and deliberate planning is an exception rather than the rule. And since psychoanalytic theory has focussed mostly upon abnormal behavior and "bad intentions", our explorations of rational and irrational aspects of such spontaneous acts should accordingly be extended into other fields of psychological research. One of the most promising avenues, then, leads us into theory and experiments on perception, and of particular relevance to our problems are, apparently, the functionalist's inquiries into "unconscious inferences" (5).

In our locomotion and manipulation of objects, we are continuously making fairly accurate discriminations of an extremely complex nature, as for instance judgments of *distance* and *object size*. Such judgments, furthermore, are *intuitive* and *spontaneous*, i.e. they follow premises and steps of inference of which we are usually not aware at all. Thus, my "immediate knowledge" of the size of an unfamiliar distant object is upon a thorough examination identified as an end-product of an unconscious inference from a variety of cues – e.g., *size of the retinal image of the object, number of other objects interspersed between myself and the distant object, texture differences in my visual field,* and so on. My accurate perception of complex physical attributes therefore frequently testifies to a nearly optimal use of information provided by previous experiences. In spite of this, however, it usually occurs without reflective consciousness.

The genuinely intuitive nature of the process, furthermore, is at times even accentuated by the individual's inability to give any coherent and adequate *retrospective account* of the inferences involved. According to careful investigations by H. O. Hebb (11), this is clearly the case in the experienced animal psychologist's intuitive recognition of emotion in chimpanzees. According to numerous anecdotes as well as scientific investigations, it also seems to be the case in "empathic" person perception. Mrs. Smith feels immediately that her new acquaintance, Mr. Johnson, is a cold, hostile and unfriendly man, but she is as a rule unable to state why.

Some of our own studies of person perception (21) aimed at a systematic comparison between the individual's opinion, his spontaneous discriminatory behaviors, and his retrospective account of the latter. One of the experiments was conducted at the University of Minnesota, U.S.A., and young men taking introductory psychology cources volunteered as subjects. Approximately one month before the experiment, all the subjects were asked to evaluate a number of personal characteristics. A series of personal traits, e.g., looks, intelligence, honesty, etc. were listed in the questionnaire their teacher asked them to answer, and they were then asked to rank the entire set of personal characteristics in the order in which they felt those specific attributes were important to know about when choosing personal friends.

In the experimental session the same male students were asked to rank a set of 12 stimulus persons in the order they would choose them as personal friends. The 12 stimulus persons were male students of their own age, and the subjects had to form their impression of each stimulus person on the basis of a picture and a brief written excerpt from his life history. Thus, each individual was simply asked to rank-order the 12 stimulus persons in accordance with his own private preference. Immediately after this rank-ordering, however, he was asked to indicate which personal characteristic(s) of the stimulus persons he felt had mostly determined his rank-ordering. In other words, a request for a retrospective account followed immediately after the discriminatory behaviors.

By these procedures we were able to assess the individual's opinion (or ideology) with respect to the importance of specific attributes in a choice of personal friends, his actual choice of friends in an experimental situation, and his own retrospective account of that choice. The 12 stimulus persons, furthermore, had been artificially constructed by combinations of pictures and written stories in such a way that *we could infer which trait(s) had determined the individual's choice from his rank-ordering.* If for instance a subject had preferred all *intelligent* to all *unintelligent* stimulus persons, irrespective of all other differences, we could safely infer that his spontaneous ranking of potential friends had been based upon their level of intelligence.

When we then examined the relationship between the individual's opinion, his actual choice, and his retrospective account of the choice, some rather interesting patterns emerged. First, we found no significant correspondence at all between ideology and actual choice: the individuals who had indicated that it was very important to take into consideration intelligence when choosing personal friends did not *in fact* choose friends on the basis of their level of intelligence more often than the others. We found, however, a correspondence between the individual's actual choice and his retrospective account. In a number af cases at least, the subject's report appeared to be a fairly adequate account of his actual discriminatory behaviors. An almost perfect correspondence, however, was obtained between *the individual's ideology and his retrospective account of his preference ranking.* In short, nearly all subjects claimed after the choice that they had paid particular attention to a trait they considered very important when choosing friends. In some cases, therefore, the retrospective account actually seemed to be most adequately described as a false, ideologically anchored *belief* about one's own action.

These findings remind us of psychoanalytic studies of rationalization, and we may even be tempted to interpret them in the light of Schafer's distinction between primary and secondary processes. The ideology and the retrospective account of behaviors were consonant, we may argue, because they both belong to the sphere of reflective consciousness and secondary mental processes. The discriminatory behaviors, on the contrary, were apparently not under the command of reason to the same extent and in the same way. In what sense, however, were they *irrational?*

Let us now consider two extreme patterns: the *"rational intuition"* revealed for instance in a hunter's inability to account for an accurate judgment of distance, and the *rationalization* reflected in a plausible explanation of a compulsory posthypnotic act. In the first case, the perceptual achievement fulfills both our proposed major criteria of rationalness, respectively *veridicality* and *optimal use of information provided by previous experiences.* In the latter case, the act is conceived of as "indifferent to logic and reality" simple because it has been "caused" by the hypnotist's command. However, when a person who has chosen friends on the basis of their level of intelligence claims afterward that he paid major attention to their honesty, should his account be interpreted as a false description of a "rational intuition" or as a rationalization of an irrational act? ?

Our findings suggest a third possibility – namely, *the rationalization of the rational intuition.* First, any clearly *systematic* rank ordering of our stimulus persons apparently presupposes subtle and complicated inferences. A ranking based exclusively on levels of intelligence, for instance, implies a sorting of all stimuli with respect to one single and abstract common component. Secondly, such a systematic strategy may upon a thorough analysis of the individual's tacit intention actually be identified as highly instrumental. If for example the individual had a strong, though possibly latent, desire for intellectual achievement and prestige, a systematic ranking according to levels of intelligence seems to be the optimal mode of behavior in view of his previous experiences and tacit behavioral goal. Additional investigation also showed that nearly all subjects with a clear-cut preference for extremely bright personal friends were overachievers, i. e., their school work was superior to what might be expected from their own intellectual ability.

If such a person in his interpersonal relations seeks out companions primarily on the basis of intuitive, though accurate, impressions of intellectual ability, a genuinely rational intuition has occurred according to our criterion of *rationalness of the instrumental act.* On the other hand, his belief that he has paid major attention to some other personal characteristic, such as honesty, testifies to a rationalization in the sense that his false ideational representation of the act turns out to be consonant with his publicly expressed self-other *ideology.* This seems to be the essence of the *"rationalization of rational intuition"* in person perception.

Discrepancies between behavioral choice and ideation testifying to "discrimination without awareness" were also repeatedly observed in recent experimental studies of person perception in Oslo (21, pp. 77). When ranking artificially constructed stimulus-persons as potential friends, the individual frequently adopts a genuinely conceptual strategy in the sense that his sorting is made with respect to some abstract personal attribute, such as intelligence or honesty. He often seems to be entirely ignorant of his own strategy, however, and as a rule he even has, immediately afterward, a particularly *poor* recall of those very stimulus details constituting the significant premises in the chain of unconscious inference underlying his spontaneous choice.

This is the usual pattern when the behavioral choice occurs after a warming-up period at the end of which he apparently feels at ease, and confident that the experimenter is simply interested in his private likes and dislikes of other persons and nothing else. In other experimental conditions, however, we tried to induce a state of dissonance and problem-orientedness prior to the sorting of stimulus persons as personal friends. This was done by introducing specific tasks in which the subject was furnished with information contrary to firmly established beliefs and expectations. The resultant "intellectual frustration", we expected, would probably enhance a state of *reflective consciousness*, i. e., a "forcing into consciousness" of otherwise intuitive processes. And this expectation was, in fact, fairly clearly confirmed. When the subjects under such conditions adopted a conceptual strategy, they were far more successful when asked to "put into words" their actual behavioral strategies, revealing a particularly *high* recall of the perceptual premises for their conceptual sorting.

If we venture to generalize from these experimental studies, then, our tentative conclusion would be that *rational intuition seems to be the rule in "relaxed" social settings*. In most of my everyday interpersonal situations, I am totally unaware of the many subtle discriminatory mechanisms involved. When inviting people to a party, when approaching another person with the purpose of making friends, etc., my seemingly "acting without foresight" may upon a thorough examination reveal consistent and rational strategies. Some such strategies may apparently be "forced into consciousness" without any serious loss other than a feeling of detachment. If I have the feeling that somebody questions the wisdom of my spontaneous acts, for instance, I may for a while become "an object to my-self": I tend to watch my own steps by keeping a continuous ideational record of ongoing mental operations.

Becoming an object to oneself, however, may under certain conditions also imply *a serious secondary process interference in otherwise efficient intuitive strategies.* Suppose I have the belief that Ethics is the supreme guide in my interpersonal relations, whereas thorough investigations of my spontaneous acts clearly testify to an ingenious intuitive strategy pivoting around Power. My deliberate attempts at "being rational" in interpersonal relations may then actually result in a peculiar and unfortunate compromise. On the one hand, the wisdom of my indecent intuitive strategy is at times ruined by success-ful and deliberate ideational control of behaviors. On the other hand, successful "power intuition" may enter my reflective consciousness in a distorted ideational form, because of my bad intention of preserving a picture of myself as an ethical person rather than knowing the truth about myself.

IX

A GENETIC APPROACH TO RATIONAL
INTUITION:
BEHAVIORAL AND IDEATIONAL STAGES
OF CONCEPT FORMATION

The repeatedly observed inability to give any adequate ideational account of systematic and "wise" strategies behind
spontaneous acts naturally directs our curiosity once more
toward certain genetic problems. Is it possible that some of
the wise intuitive discriminatory mechanisms discovered in
spontaneous interpersonal relations actually have been learned
prior to and *independently of* the ideas by which they enter
the adult's reflective consciousness?

Observations of children's social behavior seem to suggest
an affirmative answer to the above question. The small child
may begin to avoid playmates who are not telling the truth,
who fail to bring back the toys they have borrowed, and so on.
His *behavior* thus seems to testify to an ability to distinguish
between honest and dishonest conduct, between intelligent and
stupid modes of behavior, between courage and cowardice of
acts, at an age when he is still incapable of coping with the
abstract concepts 'honesty', 'intelligence', and 'courage'. A
behaviorally manifested categorization of personal attributes
is thus observed before the child has acquired the ideas in
terms of which his convictions and ideology concerning interpersonal relations are described.

In experimental studies of concept formation, furthermore,
a pattern of correct sorting behavior prior to appropriate
ideational representation of the concept has repeatedly been

observed. Because of this discovery, C. L. Hull already proposed in 1920 the term "functional concept" as a label for intuitive conceptual behavior. When an individual consistently behaves is if he knew the defining properties of a concept even though he can by no means report on or describe these properties, a functional concept is inferred. In Hull's studies (12), correct discriminatory behavior was thus observed at a stage of learning when the subject could not give any veridical description of defining properties at all. Even though he made no single mistake when deciding whether stimulus patterns belonged to the concept or not, he might give very insufficient and even positively misleading accounts of the premises and inferences involved in his correct decisions.

Strictly analogous observations have been made in a recent experiment on concept formation in Oslo (22). The subjects were asked to play at a wheel of fortune, and a complex geometrical figure was exposed prior to each loss and gain. Specific geometrical properties, furthermore, signalled loss and gain, and the chief purpose of the experiment was to examine the development of a concept of a "good" (or "bad") wheel-of-fortune figure.

In view of our findings, three separate stages in concept formation could be identified. Very soon, the instrumentally relevant aspect of the geometrical figure appeared to acquire perceptual dominance. Unexpected recognition tests showed that the "good-bad" aspect of the figure had been selectively attended to, even though the subject was still completely at a loss when trying to guess which figures were good and bad. At a distinctly later stage, the subject revealed mastery of the functional concept. He was by then able to guess correctly at good and bad figures, although he could not put into words or indicate by drawings *which* geometrical properties signalled loss and gain. Thus, in some cases, the "idea of the good figure" seemed to emerge as an ideational superstructure upon an already firmly established intuitive discriminatory mechanism.

55

When we consider these observations in the light of our proposed criteria for rationalness of acts and psychoanalytic perspectives on primary and secondary processes, we are once more forced to reconsider the role of reflective consciousness in man's acquisition of genuinely rational strategies of behavioral choice. The "insight" experienced by the subject who discovers which properties make figures good and bad *at a time when he has been guessing correctly at good and bad figures for a long time* appears in certain respect superfluous. It does not add much more to his intuitive strategy than does our hypothetical mechanical device for reflective consciousness to the computor's calculations. In order to *change* patterns of behavior based upon such intuitive strategies, therefore, more than a modification of ideational superstructure is required.

X

CONCLUDING REMARKS

At this point – at a region where psychological inquiries into rational and irrational aspects of Man seem to branch off into a largely unexplored though fascinating jungle of problems concerning intuitive knowledge – our explorations have come to an end. And instead of trying to give a summary retrospective account of our journey, we shall merely add a few concluding remarks.

Of all the apparent and genuine controversies we encountered in our excursions into irrational and rational aspects of Man, the basic assumption underlying our own explorations seems to be by far the most significant paradox. In brief, we have assumed that Reason can act as its own judge. In our search for criteria of rationalness we have even chosen as our basic parameter a *man-made machine, constructed according to a model of some superior calculus inherent in the human mind in a state of reflective consciousness.*

By doing so, we achieved little more than a systematic comparison between presumably irrational patterns of human behavior discovered in psychological studies and a somewhat arbitrary "ideal" pattern of rationalness. The comparison, however, brought into focus three major sources of irrationalness: *sin, sociability,* and *stupidity,* respectively. By expanding our explorations into acts and intuitively established cognitions, furthermore, we were brought into contact with scientific evidence testifying to the command of reason even in spheres beyond the scope of reflective consciousness and voluntary control.

When elaborating vague notions of rationalness into explicit criteria, we thus recognized some clearly ethical connotations. It may therefore be of some interest now to take a final look at our *rationalistic "ideal"* – the computor with the reflective consciousness – *from an ethical point of view.* And then a feeling of comfort and great relief fills our hearts. As human beings, we may certainly have reasons to repent our bad intentions and our tendency to comply with others. But, by the same token, we have also *ideals*, and *purposes*, and *morals*. Our poor friend the computor, however, appears to have no morals whatsoever, even though he is committing no sin at all!

In spite of – and also *because of* – his supreme intellectual inheritance from man, he has no personality and no morals. Nor has he any tendency to modify his strategies and at will surpass the limits of his inborn capacities – reminding us of another essential characteristic of his creator.

REFERENCES

1. *Adorno, T. W., et al.:* The Authoritarian Personality. N.Y., Harpers, 1950.
2. *Asch, S. E.:* Studies in the Principles of Judgments and Attitudes: II. The determination of judgments by group and by ego standards. *J. soc. Psychol.,* S.P.S.S.I. Bulletin 1940, 12.
3. *Asch, S. E.:* The Doctrine of Suggestion, Prestige and Imitation in Social Psychology. *Psychol. Rev.* 1948, *55:* 254–261.
4. *Asch, S. E.:* Social Psychology. N.Y.: Prentice-Hall 1952.
5. *Brunswik, E.:* The Conceptual Framework of Psychology. Chicago: Univ. of Chicago Press 1952 (Int. Encycl. of Unif. Science I, 10).
6. *Festinger, L.:* Informal Social Communication. *Psychol. Rev.,* 1950, *57:* 271–282.
7. *Festinger, L.:* A Theory of Cognitive Dissonance. Evanston: Row, Petersen & Co. 1957.
8. *Festinger, L., S. Schachter, and K. Back:* Theory and Experiment in Social Communication. Ann Arbor: Edwards Brothers 1950.
9. *Festinger, L., H. W. Riecken, and S. Schachter:* When Prophecy Fails. Minneapolis: Univ. of Minnesota Press 1956.
10. *Green, B. F.:* Attitude Measurment. In: *Lindzey, G.* ed: Handbook of Social Psychology, vol. *F:* 335–369, Cambridge: Addison-Wesley 1954.
11. *Hebb, D. O.:* Emotion in Man and Animal: An analysis of the intuitive processes of recognition. *Psychol. Rev.* 1946, *53:* 88–106.
12. *Hull, C. L.:* Quantitative Aspects of the Evolution of Concepts: an experimental study. *Psychol. Monogr.* 1920, *28:* no. 123–125.
13. *Hyman, H.:* Do they Tell the Truth? *Publ. Opin. Quart.* 1944, *8:* 557–559.
14. *Janis, I. L.:* Personality Correlates of Susceptibility to Persuasion. *J. Personality* 1954, *22:* 504–518.

59

15. *Krech, D. and R. S. Crutchfield:* Theory and Problems of Social Psychology. N.Y.: Mc Graw-Hill 1948.
16. *La Piere, R. T.:* Attitudes vs. Actions. *Soc. Forces* 1934, *14:* 230–237.
17. *Levine, J. M. and G. Murphy:* The Learning and Forgetting of Controversial Material. *J. abnorm. soc. Psychol.* 1943, *38:* 507–517.
18. *Mead, G. H.:* Mind, Self and Society from the Standpoint of a Behaviorist. Chicago: Univ. of Chicago Press 1950.
19. *Newcomb, T. M.:* Social Psychology. N.Y.: Dryden 1950.
20. *Nuttin, J.:* Consciousness, Behavior and Personality. *Psychol. Rev.* 1955, *62:* 349–355.
21. *Rommetveit, R.:* Selectivity, Intuition and Halo Effects in Social Perception. Oslo: Univ. of Oslo Press 1960.
22. *Rommetveit, R.:* Stages in Concept Formation and Levels of Cognitive Functioning. (Manuscr. under preparation for *Scand. J. of Psychol.* 1960).
23. *Savage, L. J.:* The Theory of Statistical Decisions. *J. Amer. Statist. Ass.* 1947, *48:* 238–248.
24. *Schafer, R.:* Psychoanalytic Interpretation in Rorschach Testing. N.Y.: Grune & Stratton 1954.
25. *Telford, C. W.:* An Experimental Study of some Factors Influencing the Social Attitudes of Students. *J. soc. Psychol.* 1934, *5:* 421–428.
26. *Zillig, M.:* "Einstellung und Aussage", *Ztschr. f. Psychol.* 1928, *106:* 58–106.